EXPANSION OF OUR NATION

MANIFEST DESTINY AND THE JOURNEY WEST

by Cynthia Kennedy Henzel

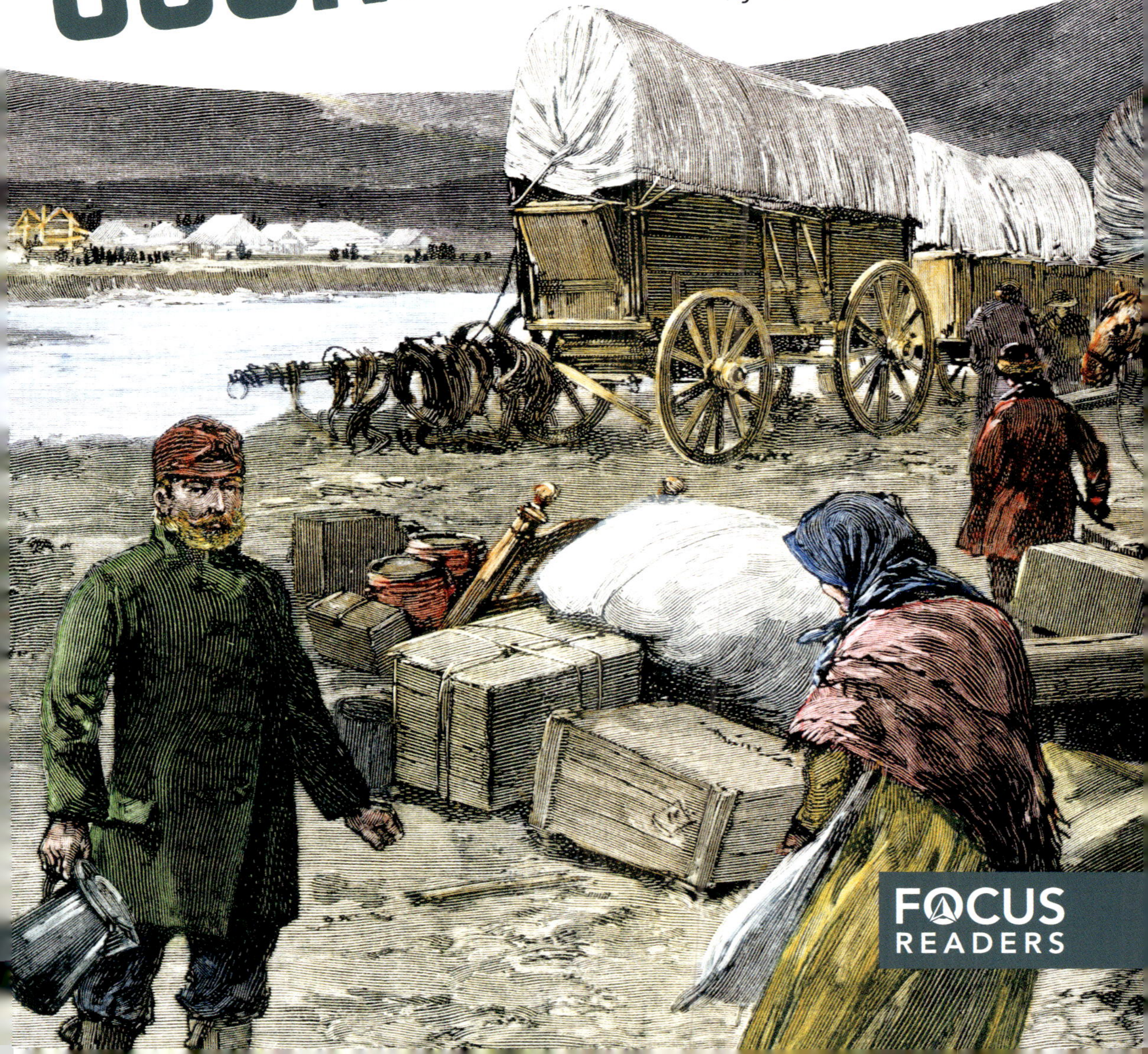

FOCUS READERS

FOCUS READERS

WWW.FOCUSREADERS.COM

Focus Readers is distributed by North Star Editions:
sales@northstareditions.com | 888-417-0195

Produced for Focus Readers by Red Line Editorial.

Content Consultant: Dr. Gideon Mailer, Associate Professor of History, University of Minnesota Duluth

Photographs ©: North Wind Picture Archives, cover, 1, 4–5, 8, 10–11, 16–17, 19, 24–25, 27, 29; Florilegius/Alamy, 7; Norman A. Forsyth/Library of Congress, 13; Red Line Editorial, 15, 21; Encyclopaedia Britannica, Inc./Library of Congress/Universal Images Group North America LLC/Alamy, 23

ISBN
978-1-63517-884-5 (hardcover)
978-1-63517-985-9 (paperback)
978-1-64185-188-6 (ebook pdf)
978-1-64185-087-2 (hosted ebook)

Library of Congress Control Number: 2018931684

Printed in the United States of America
Mankato, MN
May, 2018

ABOUT THE AUTHOR

Cynthia Kennedy Henzel has a BS in social studies education and an MS in geography. She has worked as a teacher-educator in many countries. Currently, she works writing books and developing education materials for social studies, history, science, and ELL students. She has written more than 80 books for young people.

TABLE OF CONTENTS

CHAPTER 1

A NATION EXPANDS

After the Louisiana Purchase in 1803, thousands of people in the United States moved west. Some rode in wagons or **stagecoaches**. But most traveled by water. Many people followed the Missouri River. Meriwether Lewis and William Clark had used this route during their expedition to explore the new territory.

In the early 1800s, steamboats made it easier for people to travel and settle along rivers.

However, this land was not empty. It belonged to American Indian nations. Before 1815, the US government had treated these nations like separate countries. But that began to change. **Nationalism** was growing. US leaders did not respect or value American Indian cultures. They treated American Indian land like it was part of the United States.

During the 1820s and 1830s, the US government forced many American Indian tribes out of areas where white people wanted to settle. First, tribes on the Great Plains, such as the Osage and Kansa, were forced to give up some of their land. Next, the US government forced tribes

The Osage lived in areas that would become Missouri, Arkansas, Kansas, and Oklahoma.

from farther east to move to that land. It became known as Indian Territory.

Many American Indian tribes were driven from their land near the Great Lakes. For example, the Shawnees were forced to leave their homes in Ohio. They moved west of the Mississippi River.

The Indian Removal Act of 1830 was used to force nations such as the Seminoles to leave their homelands.

Other nations soon followed, including the Chippewa, Miami, and Potawatomi.

American Indians in the Southeast lost their land as well. The Choctaws, Creeks, Chickasaws, Cherokees, and Seminoles were forced to sign a series of **treaties** and move west to Indian Territory. This new land was very different from the land they left behind. In addition, many tribes were forced to live together in a small space.

In some cases, fighting broke out between American Indian nations. Some members of the Great Plains tribes saw the tribes from the East as invaders. For example, the Osage tribe had lost hunting grounds. They fought against the Creeks, Choctaws, and Shawnees who moved to that land. Many other tribes felt their land had been taken unfairly.

Settlers rushed to the areas where these tribes had once lived. Soon, their farms and towns stretched west of the Mississippi River.

CHAPTER 2

TO THE PACIFIC NORTHWEST

By 1830, settlers had filled Louisiana, Arkansas, and Missouri. They were looking for more land. But just to the west was Indian Territory. And beyond that was the Great Plains, an area thought to be a desert. Some settlers followed the Santa Fe Trail to Texas or New Mexico. But many looked all the way to the Pacific Coast.

The Hudson's Bay Company bought and sold fur at trading posts along the Pacific Coast.

Lewis and Clark had explored part of the Pacific Coast in the early 1800s. They had reached the Oregon Country in 1805. But the journey had been long and hard. Few US settlers came to the Oregon Country. Instead, most people who came to the area were fur traders or trappers. Many worked for the Hudson's Bay Company. This British fur-trading company had many trading posts in the area. It also traded with local American Indian tribes, such as the Nez Perce, Flathead, Snake, and Ute.

In 1818, British and US leaders had agreed that people from both countries could live in the Oregon Country. But in

Members of the Flathead nation later lived on a reservation in Montana.

the 1830s, more people from the eastern United States began traveling to Oregon.

In 1831, four American Indians came to St. Louis, Missouri, with fur traders. Their visit inspired **missionaries** to travel to Oregon. Marcus and Narcissa Whitman led one of the first groups in 1836. They planned to live near the Flathead tribe.

They also encouraged settlers to come to Oregon. They wrote letters and journals describing their new home.

As news of the Oregon Country spread east, more people became interested in the area. The descriptions of fertile land appealed to farmers. Owning land was seen as a sign of wealth. Plus, the US **economy** began to struggle in 1837. In the next few years, lots of people lost money. Many decided to look for new opportunities in Oregon.

People from across the United States began moving to Oregon. Some traveled by sea. But many followed a route that fur traders had used. This route became known as the Oregon Trail. Travelers had to cross approximately 2,000 miles (3,200 km) of plains, deserts, and mountains. It was a long, hard journey. But by the 1840s, the trail was filled with wagons traveling west.

TRAILS FOR TRAVELING WEST

CHAPTER 3

ON THE OREGON TRAIL

The first group of wagons left Missouri in May 1842. A team of horses, mules, or oxen pulled each wagon. Most people walked alongside the wagons. One wagon could carry approximately 2,000 pounds (900 kg). People packed food for the trip. They also brought tools for farming and building new homes.

Wagons had to cross the Rocky Mountains to reach Oregon.

The wagons traveled in small groups. A guide rode ahead and planned the day's route. Wagons could usually go 15 to 20 miles (24 to 32 km) in one day. After traveling all day, people stopped to cook food and care for their animals.

The first wagon train reached Oregon in October 1842. News of the success reached Missouri. Even more people were eager to move. A larger group set out in May 1843. This group brought five times as many US settlers to Oregon. The settlers wrote letters home. They described the wonderful land. Thousands more people moved to Oregon during the rest of the 1840s.

Wagons on the Oregon Trail sometimes had to ford, or cross, a river.

People faced many dangers along the trail. They had to travel in rain, wind, and heat. Diseases killed many people. And wagons had to cross the mountains before winter. Otherwise, the trail would be blocked by deep snow.

Travelers met American Indian tribes. Some tribes attacked wagons or stole horses. But others helped the travelers.

Settlers often traded with them for food or supplies. On the Great Plains, the settlers hunted buffalo until there were almost none left. Many tribes in this area depended on these animals for food.

As more US settlers reached Oregon, they began to want more US government control. The British still claimed some of the land in the Oregon Country. But they realized they could not keep US settlers out. In 1846, they agreed to the boundary that separates the United States and Canada today.

Other parts of the United States were growing, too. Texas had been **annexed** in 1845. And people were eager for the

United States to grow even more. Some wanted the country to expand all the way across North America. This idea became known as *Manifest Destiny.*

THE UNITED STATES EXPANDS

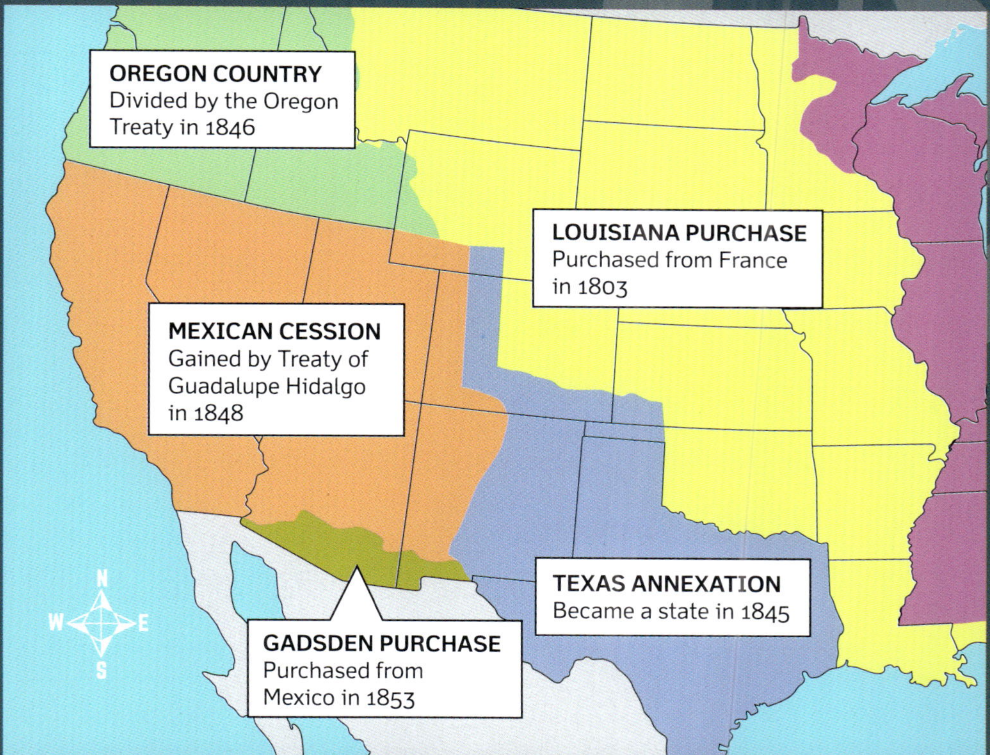

JOHN O'SULLIVAN

John O'Sullivan was a newspaper editor. In 1845, he wrote articles in support of expanding to the West. He said the United States had a "manifest destiny" to spread across North America. In fact, he thought the country should eventually "possess the whole of the continent."

Like many US citizens, O'Sullivan saw the United States as a model for other countries. He believed its form of government was the best possible kind. He called it "the great experiment of liberty and **federated** self-government." By spreading across North America, O'Sullivan wrote, the United States would bring freedom and equality to many people.

O'Sullivan originally thought people would choose to join the United States. But the term *Manifest Destiny* was also used to justify taking land by force. Some leaders claimed the United

In 1845, John O'Sullivan was the first person to use the term *Manifest Destiny*.

States was superior to American Indian nations. They used this idea as an excuse to push those nations off their land. As the United States expanded, tens of thousands of American Indians lost their homelands.

CHAPTER 4

CALIFORNIA AND GOLD

Around the time people started moving to Oregon, other settlers traveled to California. The first group set out in 1841. A few others followed, though not nearly as many as moved to Oregon. This began to change in 1848. That year, a carpenter named James Marshall found gold near a mill that belonged to John Sutter.

During the Gold Rush, one of every 100 people in the United States moved to California.

Other workers found more and more gold, and the news began to spread. Many people left their jobs to look for gold near Sutter's Mill. Even sailors and soldiers deserted their posts. The Gold Rush had begun.

News of the gold traveled east. Soon, people from around the world rushed to California. Many traveled by boat. Some sailed all the way around South America. Others crossed the Isthmus of Panama. This made the trip much shorter. But travelers had to canoe up the Chagres River and cross 20 miles (32 km) of mountains. And then they had to take another ship to California.

Travelers had to cross a dangerous jungle to reach ports on the other side of the Isthmus of Panama.

Other gold-seekers traveled by land. Many followed the California Trail, which ran through the slave state of Missouri. Many travelers from northern states had never seen slavery firsthand before.

Approximately 90,000 people had moved to California by 1849. In fact, so many settlers arrived that the territory applied to become a state.

Lawmakers debated whether the new state would allow slavery. In 1850, they reached an agreement. Called the Compromise of 1850, it was made up of five laws that tried to keep the balance between free states and slave states. California became a free state.

The United States now stretched all the way to the Pacific Ocean. But to reach this goal, the US government had pushed thousands of American Indians off their lands. US officials forced people to sign unfair treaties. They broke promises to American Indian leaders. And they would break their promises again later. The US government had said the move to Indian

During the 1800s, settlers built towns in the Pacific Northwest.

Territory would be **permanent**. They thought white settlers would not want to live on the land. But by the 1880s, that had changed. The US government opened Indian Territory to white settlers. American Indians were pushed out. Once again, the idea of Manifest Destiny was used to take land.

FOCUS ON

MANIFEST DESTINY AND THE JOURNEY WEST

Write your answers on a separate piece of paper.

1. Write a paragraph summarizing the main points of Chapter 1.

2. If you lived in the 1800s, would you have traveled the Oregon Trail? Why or why not?

3. What year did the first wagon train reach Oregon?

- **A.** 1842
- **B.** 1846
- **C.** 1850

4. Why did some people leave their jobs to travel to California during the Gold Rush?

- **A.** They thought traveling to California would be easier than going to Oregon.
- **B.** They wanted to start farms on the land near Sutter's Mill.
- **C.** They thought they could earn more money looking for gold.

Answer key on page 32.

GLOSSARY

annexed
Took over a country or territory.

economy
The system of goods, services, money, and jobs in a certain place.

federated
Formed by joining together several states, nations, or other groups.

missionaries
People who teach religious beliefs and attempt to convince others of those beliefs.

nationalism
The belief that one's country is superior to other countries.

permanent
Lasting a long time, not changing.

stagecoaches
Carriages that were pulled by horses and often carried passengers or mail.

treaties
Official agreements that are made between two or more countries or groups.

TO LEARN MORE

BOOKS

Christopher, Nick. *The Dream of Manifest Destiny: Immigrants and the Westward Expansion.* New York: PowerKids Press, 2016.

Stuckey, Rachel. *Wagon Trains Heading West.* New York: PowerKids Press, 2016.

Watson, Stephanie. *A Timeline History of the California Gold Rush.* Minneapolis: Lerner Publications, 2015.

NOTE TO EDUCATORS

Visit **www.focusreaders.com** to find lesson plans, activities, links, and other resources related to this title.

INDEX

Answer Key: 1. Answers will vary; **2.** Answers will vary; **3.** A; **4.** C